THE BAMBARA

INSTITUTE OF RELIGIOUS ICONOGRAPHY
STATE UNIVERSITY GRONINGEN

ICONOGRAPHY OF RELIGIONS

EDITED BY

Th. P. van Baaren, L. Leertouwer, F. Leemhuis and H. Buning (*Secretary*)

SECTION VII: AFRICA

FASCICLE TWO

LEIDEN
E. J. BRILL
1974

THE BAMBARA

BY

DOMINIQUE ZAHAN

Professor at the Sorbonne

With 42 plates

LEIDEN
E. J. BRILL
1974

ISBN 90 04 03963 5

CONTENTS

SELECT BIBLIOGRAPHY

BINGER, Captain, *Du Niger au Golfe de Guinée par le pays de Kong et le Mossi, 1887-1889*, Paris, Hachette, 1892, vols. I & II.

BRUN, R. P. J., *Le totémisme chez quelques peuples du Soudan occidental, in Anthropos*, 1910, vol. 5, pp. 843-869.

DELAFOSSE, M., *Haut-Sénégal-Niger*, vol. III, *Les Civilisations*, Paris, Larose, 1912.

DIETERLEN, G., *Essai sur la religion bambara*, Bibliothèque de Sociologie contemporaine, Paris, Presses universitaires de France, 1951.

——, *Mythe et organisation sociale au Soudan français*, in *Journal de la Société des Africanistes*, Paris, vol. XXV, 1955, parts I & II, pp. 119-138.

GANAY, S. DE, *Aspects de mythologie et de symbolique bambara*, in *Journal de Psychologie normale et pathologique*, Paris, April-June, 1949, pp. 181-201.

——, *Notes sur la théodicée bambara*, in *Revue de l'Histoire des Religions*, Paris, vol. CXXXV, 1949, pp. 187-213.

HENRY, R. P. J. M., *Le culte des esprits chez les Bambara*, in *Anthropos*, Vienna, vol. III, 1908, pp. 702-717.

——, *L'âme d'un peuple africain. Les Bambara*, Collection internationale de monographies ethnologiques. Bibliothèque Anthropos, vol. I, 1910.

KJERSMEIR, C., *Centres de style de la sculpture nègre africaine*, Paris, A. Morancé 1935-1938.

LABOURET, H., *Les Manding et leur langue*. Bulletin du Comité d'Études Historiques et Scientifiques de l'A.O.F., Paris, Larose, vol. XVII, 1934.

PÂQUES, V., Les Bambara. Monographies Ethnologiques Africaines, Paris, Presses Universitaires de France, 1954.

TAUXIER, L., *La Religion Bambara*, Études Soudanaises, Paris, Paul Geuthner, 1927.

TRAVÉLÉ, MOUSSA, *Usages relatifs aux jumeaux en pays bambara*, in *Outre-Mer*, 1931, vol. 3, pp. 99-102.

ZAHAN, D., *Sociétés d'initiation bambara: le N'domo, le Korè*. Paris-The Hague, Mouton, 1960.

INTRODUCTION

The Bambara number about 1.500.000 people, dwelling in the Mali Republic, in the middle valley of the Niger. They are an essentially agricultural community and live mainly on their crops of fine millet, sorghum and *fonio*.

Islam and Christianity have opened large breaches in the traditional religion of this race, but the great majority of them have remained attached to their ancestral beliefs.

These beliefs are grouped around what is generally known as "ancestor worship", together with various initiatory societies. But, seen on more general lines, these religious beliefs themselves appear to form part of a wider system in which the worship of the deity, a devotion less obvious at first sight because less well defined in the mind of the faithful, underlies all their religious practices.

In such a framework the rites and cults necessary for the spiritual life of the individual and of the village community offer many variants. These are not so much an expression of the fluctuation of religious feeling among the Bambaras with regard to their fundamental beliefs as an expression of the diverse interpretations of their attitude to the deity. They move at ease in the maze (never yet fully explored) of rites and practices wrongly described by certain writers as "superstitions" or, more "scientifically", as "animist" or "fetichist" practices. More often than not the bambara religion, like that of many traditional civilisations, has been studied only at the ground roots, and not in its highest forms of expression.

These brief observations define the main lines of our study, which must in any case be rather summary because of the limits imposed upon us.

1. *The deity and the way in which it is represented.*
The Creation

The Bambara recognise one God, supreme over all, *Ngala* or *Bemba*,[1] whose fundamental rôle is that of Creator. The other divine "Persons", *Mousso koroni koundyé* or *Nyalé, Faro* and *Ndomadyiri* (who are also the elements of air, fire, water and earth) are intimately linked with the life of *Bemba* and with his creative works but, in the created world, each of them has a particular and specific rôle.

According to a cosmogonic myth, the correlations between these four personages are already apparent before the creation of the universe, during one of the stages of the evolution of the creative spirit, properly so called. At a certain moment the First Principle, from which living beings and all things are to be formed, bears the name of *Koni*. He is thought (*miri*), and dwells in secret within the void (*lankolo*), and he himself is also this void. At this stage certain myths represent him as a whirlwind, others as a vibration containing all uncreated things in the state of signs.[2] However this may be, the Bambaras

---

[1] He has many other names.

[2] For the Bambara myth of creation cf. S. DE GANAY, *Aspects de Mythologie et de Symbolique Bambara*, Journal de Psychologie normale et pathologique, April-June, 1949. Presses Universitaires de France, pp. 181-201; *Notes sur la théodicée bambara*, Revue de l'Histoire des Religions, vol. cxxxv,

admit that from the moment when the deity begins his work of creation, this work is done in three stages.[1]

The first of these stages is called the "creation of the beginning" (*dali folo*) and represents a project that is still unorganised, a beginning made in secret, "without a voice" to express itself, a time in which the world, and man within it, are present only in chrysalis form. Even if men, animals, plants and all other things already exist, they are still formless.

In this original phase the naked earth is one of God's first creatures. God, now called *Pemba*, at first shows himself in the form of a grain (*kise*) which has issued from him. From this grain springs a tree, the *balanza* (*acacia albida*) which, when fully grown, withers and falls to the ground. There remains only a thick oblong beam, lying on the naked earth, and this is called *Pembélé*.

Alone upon the earth, the *Pembélé*, the avatar of the deity, begins to secrete a sort of mildew which forms a heap beneath it. The *Pembélé* kneads this mass with its own saliva and infuses into it a *ni* (soul or vital force) in order to form a new being of female appearance which it names *Mousso koroni koundye* (little old woman with a white head). *Mousso koroni*, becoming the wife of *Pembélé*, engenders vegetables, animals and human beings. But everything is produced in haste, disorder and confusion, in order that all that is necessary for peopling the world may proliferate as rapidly as possible.

Later on *Mousso koroni* plants the *Pembélé* in the ground, where it takes root and becomes a tree again. This *balanza* tree, called God (*Ngala*) by men who, being at that time immortal, recovered their youth through his power, was to be the cause of death. The worship offered to him was then transferred to his rival, *Faro*, the lord of water.

According to this myth *Mousso koroni* now disappears, after a wretched life in female form. However, according to many Bambaras, *Mousso koroni* is indestructible, being also a personification of the elements of air, wind and fire. She is moreover believed to be the "mother" of magic, and therefore of all transformations, and in this context she is given the name *Nyalé*, by which we also shall refer to her.

The first stage of creation is placed under the sign of this divine "Person", considered by the Bambara to be one of the three "foundations" of their religion. She deserves a rather closer study.

Having issued from *Pembélé* and been kneaded with his saliva, in order to acquire a female form, *Mousso koroni* is believed to have been originally created from the breath of *Bemba*. Being the first to possess a Soul, she is at the source of all vital principles. That is why the "faithful" represent her as pervading the whole of creation—still in a secret and shadowy way—not only in order to sow the myriad *ni*, souls, but also to sow the germs of all knowledge. Because of this power of hers certain worshippers (some sacrificial priests) venerate her in secret, imploring her, for example, to give strength to a new born infant or to hasten the ripening of the various grains. *Nyalé* is also at the source of all the ideas which have been or will be given to man, ideas which she places "obscurely" in their unconsciousness and in their memory, that is, beyond the reach of their ego. As we shall

---

nos. 2 & 3, April-June, 1949, Presses Universitaires de France, pp. 187-213; G. DIETERLEN, *Essai sur la religion bambara*, Paris, Presses Universitaires de France, 1951, chap. I. Other aspects of the myth of creation are to be found in G. DIETERLEN: *Mythe et organisation sociale au Soudan français* in Journal de la Société des Africanistes, Paris, vol. xxv, 1955, nos. I & II, pp. 43 et seq.

[1] Some of the documents consulted for this article are as yet unpublished. They belong to Mme. S. DE GANAY to whom we express our profound gratitude for having been allowed to use them.

see later on, the intervention of two other "foundations" of creation will be necessary in order that these reflections of intellectual concepts may be embodied.

This divine "Person" also represents activity, energy, impetus, secrecy and desire, for without desire there would be nothing. She also gives taste, that is, the attraction felt for certain things and certain beings, an attraction which generally hears the imprint of speed and exaltation, even of an excessive haste which, if too impatient, leads to disaster.

Moreover, all malice and misunderstanding are caused by *Nyalé*. Sorceries and transformations, as well as treachery, are associated with her.

In the minds of the Bambaras the air, wind and fire with which she is associated are the indispensable elements of the world's onward movement. But as these principles may be active in an uncontrolled, that is, unruly and often excessive manner, *Nyalé* is considered to be a profuse and extravagant being. She represents swarming life; she causes all things to proliferate, including languages which, although audible, are unintelligible.

So by her very nature *Nyalé* is, to a certain extent, a factor of disorder. That is why it is said that although *Bemba* gave her a soul (*ni*) when, under the name of *Mousso koroni*, she took a female form, he took away her "double" (*dya*) in order to entrust it to *Faro*. This was a wise measure on the part of the Creator, who wanted in this way to set bounds for the world's disorder. In fact, only the association of the *ni* and the *dya* together gives a being its coherence, its *raison d'être* and its hope of eternal life.

The second stage of creation corresponds to the process of setting the world in order. It is called *dali flana* and is placed under the sign of *Faro*, whose essential attribute is equilibrium. It is also placed under the sign of *Ndomadyiri*, who is responsible for restraint and stability.

Faro, the second divine "Person", and "foundation" of religion, is androgynous (Pl. IV). He is generally called *dyi tigi*, the lord of water, for this element is his favourite dwelling on earth. He is found also in watery vapour. In the river Niger he lives chiefly in the twenty-two *Faro tyin*; these are deep holes in the river bed, found here and there along its course. Sacrifices are offered to him in every one of these places.

In certain drawings representing him *Faro* is always shown in a female form, with breasts, long hair and a fish tail, but he may assume other forms too. His characteristic manifestations are rain, rainbows, thunder and lightning. With lightning he punishes certain infringements of taboos, whether these prohibitions concern him directly or not.[1]

But this is only one of the aspects of this divine "Person", whose dwelling in space is the seventh heaven, the source of beneficial showers of rain.

Faro is above all the "witness" of *Bemba*, the lord of creation, and so it is he who completes *Bemba*'s work and is commissioned by him to perfect the world, to organize it by setting it in equilibrium, and to give it eternal life.

Faro was born of the vaporous breath of the Creator from a bubble of his saliva, while he, the Creator, was pronouncing the creative words. He is the "word" that *Bemba* uttered. Issuing from the vaporous breath of the creative words, he is water, light, speech and life. The Bambaras also assert that although *Faro* is not the equal of the invisible Creator, he is his visible countenance; he is both the act of creation and the image of the created world, in

---

[1] Other details concerning myths and beliefs about *Faro* are to be found in G. DIETERLEN: *Essai sur la religion bambara*.

which he shows forth *Bemba*. Being the word of God, *Faro* is called the "head of all things", or sometimes the pivot, for he executes the commands of his "fulcrum".

The "word" which is *Faro*, does not mean for the Bambaras something abstract, something alien to the reality of the world around them. On the contrary: this "word" is the link connecting all things, it is like the sky which covers the earth, engendering all life; it is necessary in order that the world shall come to an understanding of itself, and it expresses its perfection.

But, to the mind of these Sudanese, *"Faro*-Word" means, at this stage of Creation, a sort of language in which the words are not separated one from another, that is to say, a language that cannot be understood.

This is why, even at this stage, *Ndomadyiri*, the third divine "Person", already makes his presence felt. For this "Person" is needed for separating and distinguishing things from one another, as well as for carrying out the breaks of the speech. It is through him that speech, as a means of communication, has become transformed into useful discourse.

Ndomadyiri is the heavenly blacksmith and also man *par excellence*. He is also the element "earth", the last of the four First Principles, and was formed by the evaporation of water (*Faro*), due to the action of the wind (*Nyalé*). In other words he is "what is left", that is, what continues to be in a certain place and in a certain state after the withdrawal of the elements with which he had previously been associated. This is why *Ndomadyiri* is also linked with the idea of fixity and of "dwelling", as also with the notion of a tree, a powerful and immobile vegetable, the source of the first human life. As he is associated with the tree one might even say he is a tree—*Ndomadyiri* is the lord of remedies and the healer, these properties being characteristic of all blacksmiths, of whom he is the eponymous ancestor.

Two essential attributes derive from these powers of blacksmith and healer with which he is credited. He is responsible for the invention of "poker work", that sort of writing which consists in inscribing sacred messages, traced with a red hot iron, in the wood of the objects he makes (hoe handles, bowls, various utensils, etc.). He is also the first to have used scarifications as distinctive marks, to have traced the boundaries of sacred places and to have taught the gestures proper to religious rites. As a healer *Ndomadyiri* is the being endowed with the qualities necessary for transmitting knowledge; he is the master of the teaching art, the first to reveal the "sciences" and "arts", he represents the norm in this vast and complicated field of knowledge. His fundamental merit from this point of view consists in showing men how to know themselves and teaching them composure, reconciliation, patience and perseverance, without which all teaching is in vain.

Faro and *Ndomadyiri* are thought to be inseparable, a notion that can be traced to the necessary relation between water and earth. The latter represents for the Bambaras true stability because, of the four elements, only earth has the property of permanence in the same state, and allows man to establish upon it a durable home. But, besides this quality of stability, the earth also contains water which it canalises and keeps within certain bounds. And without water there is no life, or form, or image. Water gives the earth its contours and is the "mirror" in which all things are reflected. It is in this way that water allows men the privilege of foreseeing the result of their labours. In fact it is by observing the quantity of rain that falls in the winter season that they can calculate in advance the amount of their crops. It means also that *Faro* perpetuates life because he preserves in water—the reflection of the sky—the "double" (*dya*) of all that exists.

The association of *Faro* and *Ndomadyiri* is seen also in the spiritual realm where they show their power in unison. They bring to fruition the ideas that *Nyalé* has placed in man's unconsciousness and in his memory, as we have already said. Swift, confused and fleeting ideas born under the impulsion of *Nyalé* are given a form by *Faro* who thus makes them perceptible to the mind. They are realised through the agency of *Ndomadyiri* who gives them a framework and ensures their permanence.

Some Bambara people believe that *Faro* is "neither the beginning nor the end but the centre" and indeed his privileged nature and situation explain his pre-eminent role. These Sudanese say that this is why in our present world *Faro* is constantly being invoked and is the recipient of so many prayers. It is also the reason why he is central to so many rites, whether these are of individual interest or whether, instead, they concern the whole community.

Certainly the role of *Ndomadyiri* is indispensable in the second phase of Creation, but his presence is particularly noticeable in the final stage of the Creator's work, that is, in the third period in which mankind is now living.

This last phase, in certain aspects, shows some progress when compared with that which preceded it. It is the stage of present realities when human beings and things confront each other. Human societies are formed and, within them, men assert themselves as individuals, with their wills and feelings, egoistic or altruistic, and as social beings. *Ndomadyiri*, in the guise of a smith, is everywhere present. He is the grand supervisor of religious rites and of all that has to do with "custom", because man's need to live in communities naturally entails a certain confusion, or at least a certain disorder. This is all the more evident because *Nyalé* now resumes her activity, after having been relegated to the background of existence, and having had no power over the established order of the second period. But now she re-appears, one might say (as we do our best to follow the workings of the bambara mind) like a dialectic factor in the world's onward march. In today's world she represents, as she did originally, activity, energy, impetus, secrecy, mystery, desire and the "taste" for all that man wants to achieve, for without this desire nothing is possible.

She is exaltation and enthusiasm in manual labour and all manual skills as well as in all mental effort. The intervention of *Ndomadyiri* is, on this plane, needed to control the extravagance of all kinds in which the human being would indulge if he were abandoned to the power of *Nyalé* alone. *Ndomadyiri*, as a norm, is there to show the *homo socialis* the limits set to his activity, which coincide with the tradition of which he is the guarantor.

Nevertheless, from other points of view, this phase of Creation is not only marked with imperfections but contains in its womb the germs of regression, of retreat. In fact, according to the Bambaras, social life is not an ideal; it is a necessity to which men must adapt and adjust themselves. These Sudanese often compare social life to a bulb of garlic: the cloves continue to cling to each other although all are equally evil smelling. It is the same with men and their communities. In short society could very easily break apart, and then man would be once more under the domination of *Nyalé*.

We see that Creation, as the Bambaras conceive it, is not only continual labour on the part of *Bemba*—for the three periods are but stages in a never-ending task—but is also a mixture of good and bad elements, like all enterprises impelled by a dynamic impulse towards a successful conclusion. The most paradoxical notion in this conception seems to be the role of *Nyalé*. Her total disappearance would suppress all activity, animation, courage and rivalry, which are the conditions of progress. Her unrestrained power would result in the breakdown of Creation. The fact is that the bambara beliefs about the formation of the universe are based on two diametrically opposed principles (*Nyalé* and *Ndomadyiri*) and at the same time introduce a third (*Faro*) destined to preserve a just balance between these two. The equilibrium thus established allows the world, which is in a state of perpetual evolution, to develop as far as possible, in accordance with *Bemba*'s plan for Creation.

Material objects representing the Creation

Two ritual objects represent these different phases of Creation. One, the *Pembélé*, (Pl. I, 1-2) as its name suggests, refers to the initial period when, in the beginning of all things, there reigned the *balanza* and *Mousso koroni* (Pl. II, 1-2), the male and female principles responsible for peopling the universe before the world took shape.

The second ritual object represents the one God in his fullness, the fourfold God, the creative Spirit that dwells alone in the invisible, that controls the three other Principles which he has engendered and which still exist in the world today: *Nyalé*, *Faro* and *Ndomadyiri*.

The balanza tree

Having been formed of the very essence of *Bemba*, while he was whirling round in space, the *balanza* (*acacia albida*) (Pl. III, 1) is no longer an object of worship among the Bambaras because they believe that this tree brought death to man. Even today, in certain villages, it is believed that death will befall any imprudent person who rests beneath its shade, for the *balanza* will have taken away his "double", *dya*. Nevertheless, some popular manifestations still show traces of the worship once offered. For example, women sometimes make to it offerings of oil of *karité*. Pregnant women are presented to it so that it may ease their birth pangs, and sometimes the placenta after delivery is hung about its trunk, as a token of gratitude for the assistance the woman has received.[1]

The Pembélé [2]

This is a rectangular block of acacia wood, kept by certain religious chiefs (Pl. I, 1-2). A replica, endowed with less significance, is to be found in many families. As an image of the original plank (see above, p. 2) this object may be used for various purposes, including use as a chopping trencher for the meat eaten by the household.

On its upper surface a hollow called "*Sele dẽ*" (little tomb) represents the grave in which a corpse is buried; the wood is marked with a certain number of notches which have various meanings.

The object itself represents the universe; its upper and lower surfaces and its four sides represent the six directions of space. The upper surface refers to the sky, the lower surface

---

[1] For more details concerning the *balanza* cf. G. DIETERLEN, op. cit. pp. 37, 38.
[2] The object and its symbolical meaning, here briefly described, have been studied by S. DE GANAY in *Aspects de Mythologie et de Symbolique bambara*, pp. 188-201.

to the earth, as matter. More precisely, this part of *Pembélé* signifies that the earth supports material life and that upon it human beings, as well as animals and vegetables, are born, live and die, to reappear at some future date. Evolution and the perpetual transformation of all things are indicated upon it by the number and arrangement of the notches. For example, the three groups, each of twenty-two grooves, on the upper surface represent (from left to right) first the "words" of Creation and therefore the Creator himself, then a reference to his future acts and finally the transmission of his "word" and power to *Faro*. The twenty-two round marks on the lower surface represent, first of all, the period of the Creation and ordering of the world; they also indicate all that remains unknown, all that is still possible, in short, the realisation of all the "words" on earth.

The initial pair, male and female, are represented by groups of three (male) and four (female)notches, and evoke the idea of birth and generation, while death is represented close at hand in the hollow of the "tomb". The juxtaposition of these two elements illustrates life, which springs anew even from the place where the corpse decays. Moreover, the fact that the object serves as a chopping trencher for the family's meat is highly significant. This food, very perishable and coming from a slaughtered animal, is there to signify man and his destiny, subject to the slaughterous knife of God. But, through the symbolism of the meat placed in contact with the wood, everyone may apply to himself the life giving power of *Bemba*. This is because, even if, in a general sense, the *Pembélé* represents the universe and its evolution, it also contains all the power (*nyama*) of the Creator himself, of whom, it is the symbol.

Often called *Ngala* (God) *Pembélé* it is also an altar which serves for mediation between man and God. It is the source of energy and wisdom, which it dispenses to human beings. Therefore it is the guarantor of the prosperity and life of the group, the guardian of its material and spiritual wealth. It is also seen as the custodian of souls (*ni*). This is why in certain villages it is laid on the body of a woman in labour, so that from the very moment of birth the infant may be animated by it and receive vital strength. This gesture reminds us that in mythical times *Mousso koroni*, who was born of a substance secreted from the body of the primordial *Pembélé*, was animated by him.

The altar is also used in a funerary rite in order to capture and keep the *nyama* (vital force) of a dead person. At the moment of a birth the object is waved over the head of the new born infant, to whom it transmits the qualities of the dead person. Moreover, in certain cases it is permitted to take away minute fragments of it when it is necessary to obtain a maximum of strength, but this custom must not be abused lest the *nyama* of the earth be diminished and sterility ensue.

The *Pembélé* is believed to be the protector of universal order, and of the harmony that must reign among men so that a word imprudently uttered may not be transformed as soon as it leaves the mouth, into a whirlwind which, tormenting the whole atmosphere, brings trouble to all living things.

The flani'da (twin's vase) [1]

This three-lobed bowl, also called the *flani kuna*, the twins' bowl, is considered most sacred. It may be carved by a smith, by special request, in *balanza* wood; in *sunzu* (*Diospy-*

---

[1] All the documentation, here summarised, relative to this object is still unpublished. It was collected by S. DE GANAY.

ros Mespiliformis), the tree of proliferation and abundance; in the wood of the kapok tree (*Bombax buonopozense*), the symbol of the soul, of the mind and of subtlety; in *sana* (*Daniella oliveri*), the symbol of long life and of esteem; in *dogora* (*Cordyla africana*) the tree of transformations, of secrecy and death/life.

This object is not found in all bambara villages; it is most frequently found in the region of the river Bani (a tributary of the right bank of the Niger). Even the priests do not all possess it. On the other hand, the parents of twins, or a female twin (at the time of her marriage) are likely to have one.

The *flani da* (Pl. VI, 1-2), carved in one piece of light-coloured wood, resembles an ace of clubs. It consists of a sort of handle widened at one end, with the other end rounded in the shape of a bowl. There are two more bowls, one on each side of this axis. Various poker-work drawings refer to the meaning of the whole *flani da*, which symbolises the one Creator, the source of all twinship, and the three Beings who issued from him to share in his work of creation and "direct" the world. Therefore the object is called "the three foundations of the world", or "the three Ways of the Bambara religion". This last name alludes to the initiatory societies: the *nama* and *kono* which are associated with sorcery and counter-sorcery and dependent on *Nyalé*, the society of the *korè* which is associated with *Faro*, and the *komo* which stands for order and is dependent on *Ndomadyiri*.

To describe the *flani da* in more detail; the handle which holds the three round basins is called the "stalk" of the world (*dyẽ kala*). Its upper end, which is widened, recalls God in his immensity; it also represents the eastward direction and the element air. The star engraved upon the wood has ten rays, one of which is much longer than the others and divides into three parts; it signifies the one-ness of the Creator (10 = 1), the source of all things. Its segments suggest the idea of sparkling rays, therefore of movement and of life, beginning with thought and reflection, for God, the breath of life, was able to contemplate himself in the light of his own spirit, in order to conceive Creation. The rays of the star form an open circle, indicating that the divine thought is subject to no bounds, and that if the universe came into being through God's own contemplation and will, then he is continuing to animate the world he has made out of his own substance. The star also means that, God being the intelligence of the world, he is the source of all movement, of time, space and all its directions, as well as of matter (the four elements) from which all is formed

The long ray of the star which divides into three small projections, each ending in a thick point, signifies that the mystery of Creation can only be accomplished on earth, and is the work of the three organising "foundations" of the created world, which are inseparably bound to the Creator. These three points correspond to the three receptacles placed in the form of a triangle, but whereas the points suggest the invisible, the receptacles represent the three "foundations" of the created world. The single bowl at the end of the "stalk" refers to the west and to the elements of fire and air. It represents *Nyalé*, the ferment of thought, the guardian of the secrets of sorcery and knowledge. The two other bowls are on the same plane because they are inseparable and complementary, being earth (north) and water (south). The one represents *Ndomadyiri* the heavenly smith, symbol of man, who fixes and marks out on the earth all that the other, *Faro*, representing water, light, speech and life, has thought out.[1]

---

[1] When facing the object, the left hand bowl refers to *Ndomadyiri* and the right hand bowl to *Faro*. An altar constructed by placing three pots in a triangular form (also representing the three "founda-

When one considers the four separate parts which compose the whole object, one understands that the Creator contained in himself the four elements necessary to life, associated with the four cardinal points of the compass for the maintenance of the universe. But when one adds to these four the three parts that resemble each other then the total of seven parts represents the male and female elements, birth and personality.

Generally speaking, this object, thanks to the various meanings it bears, may be said to embody a complete doctrine, summing up the history of Creation and of the chain of events which constitute it.

From the functional and practical point of view, the "twins' vase" is primarily intended to be used for the ablutions of a female twin when she has a child, but it may also be used to avert any kind of danger to one or several persons. A twin, male or female, may for example beg the Creator to protect, through its power, a warrior or a whole army. One can also, through its mediation, implore rainfall in time of need.

The objects of which we have spoken do not represent the whole range of material images of the deity. The smith's anvil (Pl. V, 1-2), *Faro's* calabash of water (Pl. III, 2), *Mousso koroni's* mask are also representations charged with significance for the Bambaras.

2. *Ancestor worship—Various cults*

As is the case with other African peoples, the religion of the Bambaras, in its most obvious manifestations, centres in "ancestor worship" which, when closely examined, can be seen to be of a very ambiguous nature.

Scholars who have made a special study of the bambara religion have generally spoken either of an eponymous ancestor or of a chain of ancestors, the first in the genealogical series being lost in the obscurity of time and apparently, in certain localities, figuring in the minds of the worshippers under the guise of an animal or a vegetable, unscientifically called a "totem" by Western writers.

Sometimes this animal or vegetable is only linked with the human race by virtue of a service rendered to the latter, through a human intermediary in the chain of ancestors.

At other times, and one must take into account here the fragmentation of the tribes, the ancestor is a human being who has fathered a whole series of generations which form a tribe.

The two final aspects of the problem here referred to are the two notions most commonly found today among the Bambaras. The notion of an alliance with a Being who, in a certain epoch, saved the human race, is very widely spread. It evokes an attempt, on the part of human beings, to give some service in return; the life of the animal or vegetable in question is preserved under the protection of the "taboo". Thus the *Diara*, the *Dembélé*, the *Koulou-bali*, the *Tangara* and the *Traoré*, who are among the best known bambara families, possess respectively as taboos (*tene*) the lion and the iguana (as well as the kapok tree), the black monkey (*ngoba*), the "pig deer" (*Sylvicapra grimmia*) as well as the siluroid fish and the panther, and a kind of *Bombax*, the spitting snake. All these families refrain from killing their animal "allies" and spare the trees or other vegetables which at some time or other have saved them from grave danger. But all this does not imply any worship of these animals or trees. So we see that the notion of an ancestor is for the Bambaras now associated

---

tions") is to be found, we hear, in certain *komo* shrines. In some villages twins are prayed for over three pots which bear the same significance. They are arranged like a clover leaf and hidden in the ground.

either with an eponymous relative or simply with the founder of the tribe. Nevertheless, the correlation between beneficent beings and the human group which benefits by their good deeds is important and in itself deserves careful study. In fact, such research would show that, in certain cases, one cannot exclude a connection between the ancestor and his taboo, for the former sometimes appears in the guise of the latter. Père Brun, quoting from a legend he heard at Ségou, which is found with variants at Kita and at Kayes,[1] refers to such cases. G. Dieterlen also relates that, in the mythical age, the first eight ancestors of men were transformed into birds,[2] and others became hyenas.[3]

One must however be careful not to see here a form of "totemism" in the usual sense of this notion. It is rather an attempt at defining human groups by associating them with certain animals and vegetables, an attempt which leads to the division of living beings and things into certain categories and classifications, in order to avoid confusion between groups of individuals. The organisation which results from this classification is doubly profitable for men, primarily because it enables everyone to know the place and rank assigned to him in the social scheme and secondly because, where marriage is concerned, it prevents the possibility of an incestuous union.

The veneration paid to ancestors play an important part in the bambara religion; it is however conditioned by two obligations. The first of these concerns the actual definition of the notion of these ancestors; the second concerns details of the celebration of the appropriate rites.

Here, as everywhere else in Black Africa, the distance in time between the faithful and their ancestors is a fundamental factor in the concept we are discussing. A distance of one generation suffices for a man to attain the rank of an ancestor, on condition that everything to do with the funeral ceremonies be properly organised by his descendants. Great age, bringing with it a profound experience of life, physical and mental integrity, participation and communion in the life of the group during its sojourn in time and space, the absence of any shameful disease, and natural death (accidental death is always a misfortune) are important factors in defining the notion of an ancestor. In short, the individual venerated by succeeding generations is considered by society to be a human, social and religious model whom the living must try to imitate, in order to prevent the deterioration of their conduct and the decay of their powers.

The rites of ancestor worship are very simple (Pl. XIa-XIVg). Stones, serving as altars (Pl. VI, 3-VII), mark the places where these rites must be celebrated, in lanes, village squares, fields and the vicinity of certain trees. Other places, nearer to man's habitations, constitute even more privileged settings for their celebration: the yard, the supporting pillar of the house porch, the threshold and the outer frame of the door embrasure (Pl. VIII, 1-2-IX, 2-X, 1).

The eldest of the tribe, that is, the individual nearest to the world of the departed, is the appointed celebrant of these rites because he is the indisputed mediator between the living and the dead. His "tomorrow" is already part of the past.

In spite of their apparently heterogeneous nature, the liturgical rules prescribed for the

---

[1] Quoted by L. TAUXIER: *La Religion Bambara*, Librairie Orientaliste PAUL GEUTHNER, Paris, 1927, p. 129.

[2] Cf. G. DIETERLEN: *Essai sur la religion bambara*, p. 23.

[3] Ibid. p. 141.

cults form a coherent whole, marking a sort of progression by successive degrees in their "stimulating" power over the dead. Fresh water and millet flour (or balls of coarsely ground millet), diluted in water, are emollients; they appease the dead and dispose them to help the living (Pl. XI, 1a-XIVg). These libations are sometimes intended simply as preliminaries to the offering of intoxicating food or drink; they are intended to awaken the dead. Frequently they suffice in themselves, the celebrant having no other purpose beyond that of establishing and maintaining a gentle and peaceful contact between the faithful and the departed. The spitting out of masticated kola nuts also serves as an introductory stage. Saliva is an aid to speech and so, thanks to the juice of the kola nut, speech becomes reflective, measured and restrained (the connection between these qualities of speech and the kola nut derives from the astringent property of the kola juice). By the celebration of this rite the priest makes his prayer more confident, precise and clear, and in return he expects from the power he invokes a precise and clear intervention. Millet beer is a restorative *par excellence*. The boiling of this fermented drink is believed to set the dead in effervescence; it awakens and excites them and makes them more disposed to intervene in human affairs. The offering heightens their sensibility and increases their energy; it inebriates them, producing a state of intoxication which is shared also by the living during these ritual carousals. Moreover, the state of bliss which these potions produce in the ancestors renders them more susceptible to persuasion. Under the power of intoxication the dead allow themselves to be worked upon, directed and influenced: they become docile. There would be no need to look for any other libations than this elixir which warms and appeases at the same time—but in this context blood too has an effect exceeding all that the human spirit could have imagined. This vital substance, drawn from the victim's body, brings life itself. By its means the sacrificing priest renews the very "sap" of the dead; he inspires them with new initiatives; he gives them strength, health and vigour. All the great moments of ancestor worship end in a bloody sacrifice, the victims being generally chickens and goats, both male and female (Pl. IX, 2; Pl. XLII). Their blood, which expresses the rhythm and distribution of their own span of time, represents man's will to insert his own span of time—into the rhythm of the cosmic harmony in which his ancestors repose. When they accept the offering of blood poured out upon their altars the dead cannot help feeling grateful to the living—it is impossible for them to refuse to do them a good turn.

The dasiri

The cult of the *dasiri* derives from the bonds which link the deity with the founding of the human community and its organisation, and is associated with the ground which the community occupies; literally translated, the word means the "attachment" or "fixation" of creation, and in fact alludes in this way to the first founding of the settlement.

There are four elements to consider in this cult: its localisation in space, its material support, the priest celebrant and the rite itself. Finally, at the end of this study, we shall see the significances of these ceremonies.

The Bambaras generally assert that the *dasiri* liturgy is addressed to a "spirit", the protector of the village, who they say inhabits a spring, a rock or even a tree. These assertions prove that they are at some pains to assign a given locality to the *dasiri* "mystery". This fixed point in space is one which served the community as a meeting place when the settlement was being founded. In fact when a new settlement is created the inhabitants first choose their future leader, who is to be the sacrificing priest of the *dasiri*. Then, while the dwellings are being constructed, everyone camps in the above mentioned locality, with hearths, vessels, arms and tools for ploughing. From the very first day libations and sacrifices are offered in this place chosen for the site of the new settlement and sufficiently clearly marked to avoid any future misunderstanding. This necessary correlation between the future settlement and its vertical "axis", an axis which does not necessarily pass through the village, means that every territorial community has its own *dasiri* (Pl. X, 2).

The material counterpart of this *"axis mundi"* is surprising as this may seem, an animal —that is, a mobile creature which is chosen from within certain categories considered propitious to men (the role of the diviner in this choice, as in the choice of the fixed point in space, is of capital importance): quadrupeds (she-ass, he-goat, monkey, hyena, rat, toad, lizard, crocodile [1]) ophidians (serpents) etc. The animal chosen is supposed to inhabit the place already selected. Birds seem to be excluded from this choice, and from this we see the trend of thought in this operation: the mobile, *axis mundi* is associated in the people's minds with animals capable of establishing "neighbourly" relations and "communications" with men, and these qualities are not found in the birds of the bush. The Bambaras speak of these mobile counterparts of the *axis mundi* as "mounts" of the spirit *dasiri*. They apply this name, *dasiri*, not only to the spirit himself but also to his lair and to his "mount". The animal chosen to serve as a "mount", once nominated by the inhabitants of the future settlement, enjoys total liberty; it always bears the name of its priest; no one must harm it, until the day when it is ritually sacrificed (if it is suitable for sacrifice—for not all are found suitable).

We have already said that the village Chief is also the sacrificing priest of the *dasiri*. One might add that many bambara villages practise a double system as regards the office of Chief.[2] On the one hand there is the land Chief who presides over all the business connected with the glebe or communal land; on the other hand there is the "political" or village Chief, who rules over the men, deriving his authority from the land Chief. The pre-eminence of this latter makes him the real priest of the *dasiri*; it is he who decrees all the processes concerned with the founding of the settlement, the use of the soil and sub-soil, as well as the organisation of the territorial community.

In many cases, however, the two offices are united in the same person.[3]

Every year the initial act of the founding of the settlement is recalled by sacrifices to the *dasiri*. In this way the initial "attachment" is periodically renewed. Moreover, every second and seventh year the ceremonies are endowed with particular solemnity, especially when they coincide with the rites of initiation to the *korè*. But sacrifices to the *dasiri* may be offered on other days, besides these annual festivities, on the occasion of all the labours connected with the use of the soil and sub-soil which concern the village community (agriculture (Pl. XL-XLII), hunting, fishing (Pl. XXXIX, 2), harvesting, the extraction of iron ores, kaolin, etc.). These sacrifices are made in order to ensure the fecundity of

---

[1] These are typical bambara categories.

[2] For the sake of convenience in writing we describe all this in the present tense although the social upheavals which have taken place in recent years among the Bambaras would suggest the use of the past tense.

[3] In this account we speak of the "village chief" as the personage exercizing both these powers.

women, at births, at the moment when the new born infant is given a name, at circumcision, on the occasion of marriages and deaths and the at septennial tattooing ceremonies by scarification, in times of public calamities, etc. Presiding over the foundation of the settlement, the *dasiri* is, in short, associated with all the social acts and with all village business. The victims offered are always white, because white signifies peace, concord, understanding and agreement, and is considered, suitable for such an association of ideas and for harmonious social relations. As a general rule, in the villages where initiation to the *korè* takes place, the septennial ceremonies of the *dasiri* coincide (and this is intentional) with those, also septennial, of the *korè*. On these occasions the animal *dasire* itself is sacrificed and the festival assumes the character of an "orgy". Before being sacrificed the victim is brought close to another younger animal, so that their heads touch. In this way the old *dasiri* is substituted for the younger animal, which is left at liberty, while the former's blood is poured over the altars of the *korè* and over the *dasiri* tree.

The meaning of the various elements combined in this cult is easily understood when we bear in mind the connection referred to at the beginning of our study, between the *dasiri*, the founding of the settlement and the deity. The *axis mundi*, in its two-fold character a geographical locality and a mobile *dasiri* animal, gives religious significance to the space around which the life and activity of the human community gather, and the *dasiri* cult regulates these same phenomenon considered as elements of renewal and regeneration.

In fact, the *dasiri* animal is identified not only, as has been said, with the *axis mundi* but also with the village community which is born, lives, grows and renews itself through death (death which is real for the animal and symbolical for the community) in order to attain long life. In this way men seek to ensure their social renewal (especially in all that concerns peaceful relations and a good understanding between families and individuals) without interfering with their stability in a fixed point of space. Here the role of the village Chief, the priest who offers sacrifices to the *dasiri*, is fundamental. It is through him—as the central pivot of the community—that the identification of the *dasiri* animal with the village society is realised. But he is also the representative of the deity—he is even thought to be the deity in person. Here we see all the religious implications of the *dasiri* cult. Human society is the reflection of the divine society and the renewal of the former represents the renewal of the latter. In fact, the biennial and septennial rituals are intended to commemorate the evolution of the divine Principle which being at first One only, assumed a dual form in order to become both male and female, that is, creative. In association with the *korè* rites the *dasiri* cult becomes the apotheosis of the individual and of his community, both seen in the light of transfiguration and immortality. This explains the so-called "orgies" in which the men indulge,[1] as well as the ceremonies which on this occasion accompany the sacrifice to *dasiri*.

The venerations of twins.

Of the peoples of West Africa the Bambaras are among those who express feelings of respect, even of veneration, for twins. They consider individuals born of the same childbed

---

[1] Authors who are ignorant of the religious significance of certain modes of behaviour, shocking to a Western mind, speak of "orgies". In fact, what we have here are movements and attitudes which seem licentious but are intended to symbolise man's joy when subject to intense religious feeling.

as a sort of replica of the androgynous *Faro*, that is, as "doubling" each other. The latest born is considered the elder.

As soon as he is informed of the birth of twins, their father, with his hands tied behind his back, is led to the doorway of the room where they lie with their mother. There he kneels down and implores them to bring happiness to the family and to preserve it from any evils that might threaten it. Then his hands are unbound. This rite may only be observed on the eighth day after the birth (the day when the baby's hair is shorn and he is given a name) or on the day when the first sacrifice is offered upon the altar (*sinsin*) of the twins (Pl. XVI, 1). The *sinsin* is part of the sacred objects of the family; the father of the family is always the priest.

If the household does not already possess this altar the father obtains it from another villager whose wife has already had twins and who possesses a *sinsin* old enough to be considered the "father", that is, the prototype of the other *sinsin* of the settlement. The guardian of this altar has not made it himself but is supposed to know the rites and formulas needed for its fabrication.

It may be made of carved wood, of iron or of wicker-work. If of wood or iron it is fashioned by a smith; if of wicker-work by a female winnower. It is always shaped like a short hour-glass, with very wide openings. Around the middle, that is the dividing line between the two cones, is coiled a piece of the twins' umbilical cord. The whole is fixed inside a half calabash turned upside down, with a cord passed through the bottom of the calabash so that it can be suspended, because the receptacle containing the *sinsin* is generally hung from the ceiling of the entrance porch.

The altar binds the twins in a close affection; it protects them both, as well as their mother, against the stings of scorpions.

The sacrifice to the *sinsin* consists of two white chickens, two white kola nuts, two balls of millet paste (or rice paste) diluted in water, and some millet beer. The victims' blood, as well as the libations, are poured over the umbilical cord inside the calabash—poured twice, once for each infant.

Besides the yearly sacrifice, celebrated at the beginning and end of the rainy season, at which family friends, the elders of the village and notabilities are present, the *sinsin* receives some bloody sacrifices on other occasions which concerns the twins: the clipping of the hair, the feast of scarifications, circumcision and marriage. The yearly sacrifice may be continued even after the children's death.

Many and complex meanings, which cannot be fully dealt with here, are linked with the liturgical matter and rites we have already described. Twinship, as a social and religious phenomenon, is associated with *Faro*. It expresses equality and equilibrium, harmony and the right proportions of all things, in imitation of *Faro* who, as we have already seen, has these same properties. This is why twin creatures are thought of as equals; hence also the obligation to give to one what is given to the other. But there is more to it than that. All twinship is really related to quadruple births, for it recalls *Bemba* and the three "foundations" of the world. This is what the *sinsin* altar in its hour-glass form is meant to signify; the two cones, joined at their apices are intended to express the most perfect equality that can be imagined, that is, the equality that reigns not between two individuals but between two pairs of twins. The same idea is expressed at the moment when the water of the libations is poured over the altar. The ceremonial prescribes that, with this intent, the water shall be offered in two small calabashes. The priest, taking one in each hand, crosses his arms and in this position pours the libation over the sacred object. By this procedure he represents, in the crossing of his arms, the shape of the altar as well as the divine quadruplicity (the Creator and the three "foundations").

The calabash containing the altar has its own special significance too. It represents the world or, more particularly, the sky as the reservoir of all things, as well as the inexhaustible source of wealth and fertility. Suspended to the ceiling of the entrance porch, the object seems to draw down upon the human beings the regards and favours of heaven. This calabash, one must add, is also associated with *Faro* who, as we have already pointed out, is the permanent representative of twinship on earth.

We cannot conclude this brief study without mentioning four more facts relating to twins.

When the rain does not come at the right time during the winter season, and the crops begin to wither, two twins of four of five years of age are placed in the full glow of the sun where they remain until the long awaited showers arrive. Some scholars (G. Tauxier, for instance) have seen in this custom a vestige of a human sacrifice. This does not seem to me to correspond with the facts, for the connection between twins and rain (the former being authentic representatives of the sky and having indisputed power over it) is well known to ethnologists.

When the time comes to winnow the millet grain, the twofold deity is invoked to obtain a breeze. For this purpose a mother of twins, facing the east and with her arms crossed, makes an offering of two small calabashes full of this cereal (Pl. XVI, 2a, XVII, 1-2).

The marriage of twins has its own peculiar rules. Two twin brothers marry two sisters, or two twin sisters marry the same man (Pl. XV, 1).

Finally, when a twin dies at an early age the survivor receives a wooden statuette to which is given the name of the dead child (Pl. XV, 2, 2bis). If the surviving twin receives a gift, another gift of cowrie shells is offered to the "doll". This puppet has taken the place of the dead twin, whose death is seen not as a disappearance but merely as a "removal". This is certainly the best way of asserting the permanence of life, through the example of twins.

3. *Initiatory Societies* [1]

Initiatory societies among the Bambaras constitute a most important social and religious manifestation. Undoubtedly the worship of the deity, ancestor worship and the other cults referred to in this brief account are very important, but the revelations looked forward to as the result of religious initiations, which we will now describe, are much more exciting. This is because these rites involve the whole community (excluding the women) and also concern mankind in general. Moreover they require from every individual a fervent and active participation and an effort of intelligence and understanding of the nature of the human being and of the destiny reserved for him by God.

In order to understand the meaning of these assertions we must take into consideration the fact that these initiatory societies constitute an organic whole. The mysterious truths

---

[1] Concerning the initiatory societies cf. our treatise: *Sociétés d'initiation bambara: le N'domo, le Korè*, Paris—The Hague, MOUTON & Co., 1960. Here the two above-mentioned brotherhoods are treated in detail, and the other four brotherhoods more summarily described.

they claim to reveal are made known by gradual stages, and the neophytes may not request to be admitted to the "higher" mysteries until they have been introduced to the "lower" mysteries of the initiatory ladder. This ladder has in all six rungs.

The first consists of the brotherhood of the *n'domo* (Pl. XVIII-XXII). It is open only to children, before circumcision (Pl. XX); they are its organisers and celebrants and therefore their function is full of significance. As they occupy an initial position within the process of the development of the individual, it naturally falls to them to express and "define", through the rites of their society, the problem of the origin of man and of his status. This task may seem extremely difficult. But the underlying idea is that only the child can usefully "discuss" that which concerns the childhood of mankind. Two notions have now become obvious. The first is the important role assigned to the child. At a very tender age he is already taken seriously and considered capable of discharging some functions which in other societies, such as our own, would be assigned to adults. The second concerns the pedagogic system itself. The teaching given by the *n'domo*, addressed particularly to the children but indirectly also to the adults, is imparted by "actors" more capable than any others of playing the role of the personage they represent: the primordial man (Pl. XVIII).

They represent the human being as he was when he left his Creator's hands, uncircumcised, androgynous, that is, possessing in one person the male and female characteristics which were later on to be separated, in order that the individual should be directed to the search for his social sexual partner. He was exemplary—that is, he possessed in himself all the good qualities that can be imagined or desired. In fact, he was a sort of "natural" man, before he was fashioned as an individual and, as we should say, stamped with the mark of civilisation. But this *homo naturalis* does not possess all the qualities required for perfection: he is "stained" with a congenital vice which these Sudanese call *wanzo* and which consists mainly in an inner blindness of the human mind in all that regards self knowledge, but refers also to physical malformations, impurity and evil in general.

In fact, the work of the six initiatory Societies is directed mainly to the effort to free man from his *wanzo*. But it is chiefly the first and the last (*korè*) of these six *dyow* (plural of *dyo*, bambara name for initiatory societies) which undertake this work and pursue it to the end. The *n'domo*, for example, does this through its internal organization which consists of five classes graded according to the progressive revelation of man and of knowledge. Each of these categories bears the name of an animal represented by an emblem.

In ascending order of importance these *n'domo* classes are: lions (*dyaraw*), toads (*n'toriw*), birds (*konow*), guinea fowl (*kamiw*) and dogs (*uluw*).

The "Lions", the entrance class to the brotherhood, are the guardians of its "great secrets" and are charged with ensuring their transmission to their pupils at the time of initiation. These "great secrets" are revealed with the aid of the *dyaraw* emblem, also called a lion. It is a small wooden rhomboid which the children of this class spin during the festivals of the brotherhood. The object represents the human spirit, which explores knowledge and strives to attain it. And as the spirit is, after all, a fragment of the deity, so the children themselves, manipulators of the rhomboid/spirit, are human images of the Creator.

The "Toads" are placed under the protection of a tailless batrachyan, symbol of the death and resurrection of man.

The "Birds" are associated with all winged creatures, considered as aerial animals. The corresponding emblem is a reed pipe which the initiates use as a musical instrument to accompany their songs. By means of this initiatory class the *n'domo* can now begin to discuss the subject of the spiritual principle which "dwells" in the body of a person, just as a bird dwells in its cosy, sheltering, nest.

The "Guinea fowl" through the gallinaceous bird of this name and with the aid of their emblem, composed of a hoe handle and a door key, have symbolic associations with the sun and the earth. This *n'domo* class sets man the problem of his first contact with the outer world, which occurs when he starts to till the soil.

The "Dogs", the last class of *n'domo* initiates, represent human beings on the plane of social relations. Their emblem, made from a perforated gourd which is spun like a rhomboid and is thus made to imitate the barking of a dog, represents human society (the holes in the gourd). The whole ensemble (initiates and emblems) explains that the community is already there, ready to receive into its bosom the solitary man of the *n'domo*.

The five classes of the society we have been speaking of offer a general outline of the problems raised by the study of man. In their own way, these categories of the initiated and their emblems suggest the creation of man and above all, the birth of his spirit ("lions"); death and life ("toads"); the totality of spiritual realities which form his thought ("birds"); man in his relations with the cosmos ("guinea fowl"); and finally man as a social being ("dogs").

When the children leave the *n'domo* brotherhood (where they spend five years: one year for each initiatory "class", the oldest pupils being replaced by newcomers), they are circumcised, which means that they are now relieved of their androgynous nature, by the removal of their female element (represented by the foreskin) and directed towards the search for their social partner (woman). It is now that another initiatory brotherhood takes charge of them: the *komo* (Pl. XXIII-XXIV).

A Bambara cannot speak of the *komo* without a feeling of awe, or even of terror. That is why he generally speaks of it in a low voice, when he cannot be overheard by his fellow villagers. The fear inspired by the *komo* is caused by its association with human knowledge.

All that concerns this subject smacks of a kind of defiance, an attitude of provocation which knowledge assumes towards all who seek it. Through the *komo* knowledge reveals itself, sometimes as seductive and pleasing, sometimes as rough and repellent. It is nevertheless always ready to confound the hypocrite and the liar, to unmask the vain and to silence the proud. And as no mortal, not even the wisest, feels totally immune to these sentiments, knowledge is for everyone a source of apprehension.

Knowledge, as explained by this initiatory society, may be considered under four aspects, through the four fundamental *komo* each of which expresses it from a different point of view. This is what the Bambaras mean when they talk about the *komo* "mothers". Everyone of these "mothers" has a certain number of secondary '*komo*' called "children". These complete and expand the idea expressed by their respective "mothers". The "*komo*" all together thus form an immense institution which, at first sight, seems to lack a properly so called hierarchy. The only obvious hierarchy is that which orders the relations between a "mother" and her children, or between a "child" and the swarms to which it has given birth.

The first *komo* "mother" (first in the order of the revelation of knowledge) bears the name of *"se"* (foot) and represents the beginning of knowledge. The foot is in fact the symbol of a beginning, an advance, of success and power. As the foot enables a man to walk, to move forward, and to make progress in space, so the *"se"* teaches all that concerns the access to knowledge and the progress made in its pursuit.

The second *komo* "mother" is called *sutoro* that is, the "corpse fig-tree". The *toro (ficus graphalocarpa A. Rich)* symbolises germination proliferation and re-birth. The name *sutoro* alludes to the funerary custom, observed by the Bambara, of burying a branch of this tree with the dead, to represent re-birth. This "mother" represents enlightenment, and teaching by demonstration, for since the principles of a truth (like the corpse resting in the ground) are lost in obscurity, to prove an assertion is like bringing these principles back to life.

The *komo* "mother" called *tamla* (flame) indicates the numinous character of know-ledge. It signifies also the illumination and excitement which the mind feels at a certain moment during the acquisition of knowledge.

Finally, the "mother" called *karangara* "to bring unhappiness", suggests the idea of suffering caused by knowledge, for this *komo* sees knowledge as a torment for those who seek it. In fact, the wise man who wishes to reach the summit of knowledge in order to enjoy it in tranquillity, deceives himself greatly, for knowledge is boundless, and the search for it is endless. The scholar might be tempted to believe that he could penetrate beyond knowledge, this is a vain hope: nothing can go beyond it. The acquisition of knowledge and man's attitude to it constitute for the Bambaras one of the most serious problems in the initiatory stage, for it is at this level that the Society judges its young members. Its judgment takes into consideration first of all their power to comprehend things in thought, as well as their capacity to guard the secret of the truths revealed to them.

Once introduced into the mysteries of knowledge, the young neophytes find themselves after a certain time (a year or sometimes even longer) constrained to face the problems of generation, marriage and society. On the moral plane they must be instructed in the distinc-tion between good and evil, because this is necessary knowledge for all who live in a community.

This problem, however, is not discussed in its more profound aspect, but considered chiefly in its relation to eugenics and to social consequences brought about in the struggle against "sorcery", changes produced by the elimination of inauspicious conditions relative to the reproduction of human beings. The initiatory society called the *nama* is responsible for this part of the training of the individual.

In a general way we might say that the *nama* (Pl. XXV-XXVII, 1) is particularly concerned with certain "relations" between various individual human beings, relations considered as an organic whole and conceived after the model of heterosexual associations. One can also say that the *nama* deals with the proliferating "unions" of "societies" and, *vice versa*, with the hostile manoeuvres which aim at destroying these unions by the art of sorcery.

This explains certain characteristic features of this brotherhood: a) the fact that the collection of objects used by the *nama* for instruction are always preserved in a bee-hive (the home of the best regulated of all communities, according to the Bambaras); b) the return of all the women to their native villages at the time of the feast of the brotherhood (in this way the community, "undone" by the departure of its women at the time of their marriage, is made whole again c) the fact that the *nama* possesses two masks, one male and the other female (Pl. XXV, 1-2), and that the former (which during initiatory ceremonies rushes in pursuit of the "sorcerers') is cut in such a way as to symbolize the vision from which no cunning ruse may escape.

The most spectacular teaching of the *nama* is expressed in the struggle against sorcery (Pl. XXVI, 1-2). A great effort is made to unmask any deceitful scheming which aims at harming the community. During the pursuit of the "sorcerers" the initiators discover the instruments used to impose subjection and constraint (Pl. XXVII, 1).[1] It is said that the "sorcerers" fashion these in order to exact submission from all those whom they wish to enslave. Deliverance from these instruments of misery is enacted by burning them under the satisfied gaze of the villagers.

The initiates of the *nama* undoubtedly learn within this brotherhood a whole set of notions indispensable for their preparation for marriage; they also learn a series of social codes necessary to the communal life which they will have to live.

With these approaches already opened, it is easy to enter the realm of the morality and conscience of the human being. The *nama*, as we have already said, touches upon this problem without examining it in detail, for that is the work of *kono* (Pl. XXVII, 2-XXVIII, 3), the fourth initiatory society in the order envisaged by the Bambaras.

The *kono*, as we shall see, adds to the flow of knowledge dispensed to the neophytes with its own contribution of very different material. It teaches the nature of man, a dual nature composed of spirit and body; it is the *dyo* of the judgment and knowledge which everyone possesses about good and evil. It reveals to the initiated, by means of the songs which are always chanted when the mask (Pl. XXVII, 2) makes its appearance, how self knowledge may lead to satisfaction or to remorse, and how the "interior voice" commands or forbids such and such an action. All this knowledge is imparted quietly and softly through a reed pipe, the nasal sounds of which are wisely thought to represent the way in which the voice of conscience is heard—for conscience, although a confused "voice" (like a half smothered warning note), does not cease to importune its owner by showing him the right way to behave in all the various circumstances of life. In order to reinforce these notions, the *kono* mask, representing an elephant (symbol of intelligence) and a bird (symbol of the spirit), lays great stress on the organs of hearing. The size of the ear flaps is deliberately exaggerated in order to underline the function and exercise of this interior "sense" of hearing, and the varying degree of acuteness of perception of man's "interior" sense influences the decisions he may make for good or evil.

With his singing and general behaviour the *kono* mask also celebrates man's capacity for thought. The union between thought and body is conceived in the form of a marriage, but whereas the material element in this association is held in scorn, thought and spirit are exalted and described with striking, even exaggerated, comparisons: thought is a "bird capable of lifting an elephant and carrying it away".

From all this instruction a Bambara certainly receives the best possible training for life in his own social environment. It would, however, be very odd if an agricultural race was

---

[1] In fact these objects are made by former initiates and hidden in places known to those who seek them. This artificial representation of the anti-sorcery struggle forms part of the teaching system used in the brotherhood. There is nothing deceitful about it.

to be without some initiatory brotherhood relating to the agricultural labour which conditions its very existence. The *tyiwara* (Pl. XXIX-XXXI) is there on purpose to meet such a need.

The *tyiwara* society, unlike the other *dyow*, is open to women as well as to men; everyone may belong to it. But only men and circumcised children are admitted to certain parts of the initiatory rite (in particular, those concerning the significance of the tools used in farming, of the properties of the soil, etc.). This open-ended character of the *tyiwara* is far from being fortuitous. Like agriculture, which is essentially day labour, everything in this society must take place during daylight hours in the sight of everyone.

From what we have already said, it is easy to deduce that the *tyiwara* intends, through its teaching, not only to train the initiates in the physical and moral qualities of all good husbandmen and in all the knowledge relating to crops and instruments of labour, but also to teach them the most profound significance of the two cosmic realities, the sun and the earth. For all farm work needs the co-operation of the sun and the receptivity of the soil.

But we must not believe that the sum of knowledge dispensed by the *tyiwara* consists in a sort of vague apprenticeship in the traditional agricultural techniques, and the teaching of some truths about the sun and the earth. This society deals with all that concerns man's food: the creation of man's settlements and the beginning of agriculture, the movement of stars and seasons, the flora and fauna, iron and the technique of making farming tools, clothing and adornment, the knowledge of poisons and, finally, the "science" of the mastery of celestial fire.

This *dyó* deals with all the realities because it is the synthesis, on the one hand of man as a manual worker and on the other hand of the facts about corn and food.

When it is considered as part of the whole organisation of the initiatory societies, the meaning and rôle of the *tyiwara* becomes even more evident. The four brotherhoods we have already spoken of were concerned with man and his community; the *tyiwara* reveals to him the extent of the cosmos. So, finally, the *korè* (Pl. XXXII-XXXVII), the last of the six societies, may reveal to him the incomparably vast space in which evolve his communications with the deity.

It is not easy to understand the significance for the Bambaras of the *korè* in the life of the individual unless we have grasped the following truths:

a) the mystical life now open to all the *korè* initiates is prepared and sustained by the training they have received in the five other initiatory societies; one of them, the *n'domo* is indispensable as a means of access to the mysteries of the *korè*, because it teaches self knowledge, and this knowledge is the prerequisite of the knowledge of God.

b) The work of the *korè* is unintelligible if it is isolated from the doctrine of re-incarnation, which can be summarily defined as teaching that the human being is, under certain conditions [1] destined to undergo endless re-incarnations. But, without the help of the *koré*, every time he returns to earth the reincarnate person is shorn of a portion of his spiritual nature, which God removes from him and keeps in heaven. It follows that the "natural" man (who is not initiated into the *korè*) dies and is reincarnate a certain number of times, until the deity has entirely reabsorbed him and refuses to give him up. It is to avoid

---

[1] We have already referred to these conditions when we were defining the notion of ancestor; only those individuals who fulfil these conditions may claim re-incarnation as understood here.

this difficulty that the *korè* seeks to "divinise" the man during his lifetime, that is, to endow him with a nature that will assimilate him to God. In this way, by usurping God's own prerogative, man may undergo endless reincarnations.

But this outcome in its turn depends on a preliminary process, the symbolic death of the initiate, a death which is to teach him that bodily death does not mean suffering and finality; on the contrary, it means union with God.

This understood, we must now look at the technique required for man to achieve the assimilation with God which the *korè* offers him.

The processes by which the institution attains the desired end may be divided into two categories: those which occupy the training period of the initiates and those which concern their awareness of their ascension towards God.

The first process is dominated by the ideas of death and resurrection, and in their initial stage follow a pattern which corresponds to the anti-natal life of a human being (a period which runs, according to the *korè*, from conception to the first moments after birth) and, in a later phase, correspond to the rites which take place between birth and the end of the ceremonies of circumcision.

The second process is a thorough training to prepare them for the mystical life. This aspect of the spiritual life of the neophytes is seen in their distribution among the eight classes of the *korè*, of which they become members. Both these two initiatory periods are divided into stages marked by particular tests.

The training period of the initiates.

From the first day of their admission to the *korè*, the neophytes are completely isolated from the other villagers. This atmosphere of separation and isolation is already the prelude to their symbolic death. Among the most common ordeals we mention: the placing on each candidate's tongue of two knives, one made of iron and the other of wood; "burial" under a hide sprinkled with irritating substances; walking on burning cinders; passing under an arch; a short stay in a straw hut. The iron knife is supposed to "kill" them, whereas the wooden knife is supposed to endow them with the germ of life, that is, of resurrection at the right moment. The "torture of the hide" represents burial in the grave as well as their return to their mother's womb (the hide is considered to be both shroud and placenta). The walking on hot cinders represents a purification and a renunciation of personal preferences. The passing under the arch (symbol of the sky) recalls the obligation, assumed by all the neophytes, to seek the knowledge of God. Finally, the sojourn in the straw hut represents the "smoke-drying" of the candidates, who thus become "food" for God (the straw hut is the celestial kitchen).

Some days after this symbolic death there is celebrated the rite of the "resurrection" of the initiates, in imitation of a birth—This initial stage of life, with the ablutions and insufflations performed upon the person of the new human being, is interpreted by the *korè* in a wholly spiritual way. Here also the neophytes submit to aspersions, ablutions and insufflations, but all with the aim of teaching them to desire and enjoy communion with the Invisible, and to arouse and refine their senses by contact with the realities of heaven.

In the first phase of the training period the *korè* initiates are, like all new born infants, in the hands of those who are looking after them. During the next stage they acquire a certain independence, resembling the freedom enjoyed by the infant after the severance of the umbilical cord. But the great events of this stage are the liberation of their souls (*ni*) and the incarnation in them of the "ancestor" that is, of God. Finally, like newly circumcised children, they are expected to renounce a state of ignorance in order to attain the stature of a perfect man, healed of his incapacity to comprehend spiritual matters.

Intensive training for the mystical life.

A *korè* "child", as the Bambaras call a *korè* initiate, does not become "deified" by a special grace, without any effort on his own part. The institution to which he belongs expects him to work very hard to advance along the road he has set out to follow. These "spiritual" exercises are undertaken in that particular *korè* class to which he is permanently assigned (here, unlike the custom of the *n'domo*, the members remain all their lives in the same class).

The eight classes of the *korè* are like a series of steps which exhibit gradually the depth of religious experience.

The "monkeys" (*sulaw*) indicate the *korè* initiates' awareness of his own animality. He must always bear in mind that in spite of his "transfiguration", he does not cease to share with the monkey an animal nature, and this thought encourages him to redouble his enthusiasm in the quest for the knowledge of God.

The "whipmasters" (*bisa tigiw*) (Pl. XXXIV-XXXV) represent the mastery of the word which *korè* initiates, in contrast with ordinary mortals, must possess. For command of speech means perfect control over one's tongue, that is, in the final analysis, absolute self-control.

The "*hyenas*" (*surukuw*) (Pl. XXXII, 1), by means of their emblem of this gluttonous animal, remind the initiates of the stability and equilibrium that characterise a man who can control his passions and is not inquisitive or greedy or insatiable.

The "fire-bearers" (*tatuguw*) represent the illumination and purification of the spirit. The fire referred to here is the deity who "inflames" the initiate and liberates him from all his prejudices, thus making him fit to serve as a guide to his fellows.

In the general plan of the *korè* these first four classes form a sort of spiritual training school which, without being set apart from the classes which follow, belongs to the "lower" plane of spirituality because it requires effort and ascetism.

The four stages which follow symbolise the union and inter-communion of man with the Invisible.

The *korè* "vultures" or "horses" (*korè dugaw*) represent the spiritual joys and pleasures experienced by those who reach the stage of union with God. These feelings are expressed by the initiates of this class in a very free, even lascivious, mode of behaviour. The liberty enjoyed by a *korè duga* (Pl. XXXII, 2-XXXIII) sets him free from all social conventions: nothing is forbidden him; for example, he may even eat human excrements as food.

The "battereds" (*kurumaw*) indulge in the spectacular habit of tearing their flesh with thorns (hence the name, which refers to the scars left by their self-inflicted wounds). They represent God taking possession of his "bride", the initiate, and the deflowering to which she submits. The self laceration is also understood by these neophytes as a self-sacrifice without which the spiritual life would be barren.

The "lions" (*dyaraw*) represent the nobility, justice and serenity of God. They signify also the royal prerogatives of everyone who has become a "bride" of God.

The "plank bearers" (*karaw*), who derive their name from the long planks which they exhibit during the ceremonies of the society, are the last and most important class of the *korè*. They express the idea of the identification of the initiated with the Invisible. The planks which they proudly present to the public and which symbolise the deity, also express the intimate union of the initiated with God (Pl. XXXVII, 1-2).

This is, indisputably, the culminating point of the *korè* mystical experience, a process which, however, as far as we can see, includes no ecstatic trances, but offers the result of the long series of exercises which the initiates have expressed in these rites, that is, conformity with an invisible model.

Two fundamental features mark this mystique. Throughout the whole of his spiritual life in the *korè*, the neophyte behaves in a manner one might aptly describe as a return to infancy. He is full of jests and jollity (this is especially the case with the *korè dugaw*), and brimming over with interior joy. Over the same period the denial of pain and death also plays a part in the initiate's behaviour. This sublimation of suffering and of the notion of annihilation is, as is now clear to all, a consequence of the initiate's awareness that he no longer belongs to the "race" of mortals, but to the "race" of the Invisible, the only being endowed in his own nature with immortality.

One must not, however, believe that the mystical life of the *korè* isolates the initiates of this brotherhood from common folk (all the initiates consider themselves to be "noble") or makes them lose the sense of every day reality. The experience they undergo changes nothing in their daily life; instead it enriches it with a new dimension, without which the future of mankind would seem to them reduced to miserable proportions.

On the religious plane the *korè* is a vast enterprise intended to improve the human condition. But it is not only that. On the social plane it is a powerful factor in the re-ordering of society. On the occasion of the septennial Feast of the brotherhood the founding of the settlement and its divine origin are celebrated in the *dasiri* rite (cf. p. 13) which reminds the villagers that all men are dependent on God. By means of other *korè* rites, they are able to beg for opportune showers of rain; by means of these ceremonies, performed on the market square, the *korè* re-awakens in the minds of all present the notion of their membership of the great human society. For all these reasons initiation into the *korè* is more than a mere religious exercise; it creates human solidarity.

Of the six initiatory societies, the *korè* is that which constitutes the climax of man's knowledge and religious instruction. It is, nevertheless, intimately allied to the *n'domo* which serves as its introduction. This is why the two societies are inseparable and no one can be received into the *korè* without having first passed through the *n'domo*. The latter is also the gateway to every one of the religious societies for, in embryo, it contains them all; like the child who is already an adult in his inceptive age, the *n'domo* interprets in its acts and gestures the initial action of the five other societies. Thus, the six initiatory societies constitute a magnificent whole, perhaps unique in all West Africa.

If we wished to summarize the bambara religion, as we have described it here, we should have to credit it with this dominant idea which runs like a leitmotiv through all its various institutions, that is, man's determination to rise above himself. Within the framework of this religion man expands like a kind of ferment (which tends to dilate its own volume in order to assume even greater dimensions) until he raises himself to the level of cosmic reality.

On the debit side of this account we must put the great mass of religious events, rites and institutions which it has been impossible to describe in this short thesis. We think, for example, of all that has to do with the personal actions of heads of families, of the individual *boliw* (portable altars), of the smith and his forge (the anvil plays an important part in the swearing of oaths), of the "passage" rites, agrarian rites, of those which are concerned with hunting and fishing, of certain masked dances (usually performed at night), and finally of the crossroads (Pl. XXXVIII-XXXIX, 1), a privileged space which the comings and goings of people unconsciously create for themselves, but which becomes sacred as soon as it is seen to be a means of orientation.

If we had been able to pursue these studies further, we could legitimately have claimed not only that man, through his spiritual life, seeks the transformation that takes him to the confines of the universe, but that the very space he occupies follows him through his various transformations and his gradual development. In this religion every personal triumph is accompanied by an enlargement of the vision of space, as if the soul were continually striving to cut out for itself wider horizons, commensurate with the ever loftier plane to which it has raised itself.

LEGENDS TO THE PLATES

Plate I, 1-2

Pembélé, representation of the deity and of the universe (cf. pp. 6-7). The upper surface (no. 1) represents the sky, the Creator and his creative "words". The evolution and perpetual transformation of things are indicated by the number and arrangement of the marks engraved upon it. We notice particularly the *sele dẽ* (little tomb), a long hollow (in the middle, coloured black) which represents the part of the tomb where the corpse is placed and signifies death and resurrection. The lower surface (no. 2) represents the earth, as matter. The twenty-two round marks represent the time appointed for the creation and organization of the world as well as the realisation on earth of all the creative "words".

Provenance: Ségou region, Mali Republic. Dimensions: 0.80 m × 0.10 m. Material: wood of *acacia albida*. Collection: Madame S. de Ganay.

Plate II, 1-2

Mask from the *Do* ritual of the village of Pélenguéna. Worn during certain nocturnal dances, it represents *Nyalé* (or *Mousso koroni*), one of the three "foundations" of creation (cf. pp. 2-3, 5-6), in the form of a bovine animal.

Provenance: Pélenguéna, Mali Republic. — Dimensions: total height 1 m . × 0.50 m. — Material: wood of kapok tree. — Photographed by Madame S. de Ganay.

Plate III, 1

Balanza tree, scene of sacrifice to *Mousso koroni*, in the Ségou region (Mali Republic). For this sacrifice the tallest tree is always chosen. Photographed by Madame S. de Ganay.

Plate III, 2

Calabash of *Faro* water in the Ségou market. The smaller calabash serves to scoop up the drinking water from the large receptacle.

Provenance: Ségou, Mali Republic. — Dimensions: diameter of large receptacle 0.50 m., diameter of small receptacle 0.20 m. — Material: Fruit of the calabash plant. — Photographed by Madame S. de Ganay.

Plate IV

Ritual axe representing androgynous *Faro*: the male element by the cutting edge, the female element being on the opposite side.

Provenance: Mali Republic. — Dimensions: length 0.50 m., diameter of the handle 0.04 m., width of the cutting edge at the top of the personage's head 0.30 m. — Material: wood. — Private collection. — Photographed by the *Musée de l'Homme*.

Plate V, 1

Anvil, against which a smith is leaning, in imitation of the attitude of the king before his departure for war. The anvil of the forge serves as an altar; oaths also are sworn upon it.

Provenance: Kalabougou, Mali Republic. — Photographed by Madame S. de Ganay.

Plate V, 2

Anvil, common property of the smiths of Kalabougou, Mali Republic. Photographed by Madame S. de Ganay.

Plate VI, 1-2

The "twins vase" (*flani da*) (cf. pp. 7-9). Representation of the Creator and of the three "foundations" of Creation.
Provenance: Bani Region, Mali Republic. — Dimensions: 0.54 m. × 0.30 m. — Material: wood of kapok tree. — Collection: Madame S. de Ganay. — Photographed by Madame S. de Ganay.

Plate VI, 13

Ancestor's stone in the Ségou region, Mali Republic. (For the illustrations Pl. VI, 3-XIV cf. pp. 9-11).
Photographed by Madame S. de Ganay.

Plate VII, 1-2

Ancestors' stones at Sama, Mali Republic. These altars are here fixed in a block of masonry, beside the entrance of a dwelling.
Photographed by Madame S. de Ganay.

Plate VIII, 1

Little "building" dedicated to ancestors at Kalabougou, Mali Republic. The altar, built of mud, is near a pond sacred to *Faro*.
Photographed by Madame S. de Ganay.

Plate VIII, 2

Altar sacred to ancestors, Mali Republic.
Photographed by Madame S. de Ganay.

Plate IX, 1

In the market of Ségou, Mali Republic. Grains, fruits and besoms used in certain rites relating to ancestors.
Photographed by Madame S. de Ganay.

Plate IX, 2

Libation of millet gruel and the sacrifice of a chicken to ancestors, to the right and left of the entrance door of a dwelling.
Provenance: Ségou region, Mali Republic. — Photographed by Madame S. de Ganay.

Plate X, 1

Entrance door of a smith's house with traces of a bloody sacrifice on each side of the portal.
Provenance: Konodimini, Mali Republic. — Photographed by Madame S. de Ganay.

Plate X, 2

Dasiri tree and animal (cf. pp. 11-13).
Provenance: Ségou region, Mali Republic. — Photographed by D. Zahan.

Plates XI-XIV

At Pélenguéna, Mali Republic. Different stages of the offering (fresh water, millet gruel and kola nuts) made to ancestors before the entrance door of a dwelling.

(a) During the invocation the priest (the eldest of the lineage) holds the bowl of fresh water in his right hand and the bowl of millet gruel in his left.
(b) Some of the fresh water is poured out (at the bottom of the bowl may be seen two kola nuts).
(c) A little of the same water is poured into the bowl containing millet gruel.
(d) The priest pours the millet gruel over the fresh water.
(e) He dips a kola nut in the libations already offered.
(f) He crunches with his teeth a bit of the kola nut.
(g) He spits this out on to the libations already offered.
Photographed by D. Zahan.

Plate XV, 1

Every young Bambara girl ceremoniously receives, at the time of her marriage, a wooden basin in which she places her soap for personal washing. The double basin here shown is intended for a twin girl, in order that she herself may give birth to twins. She keeps the soap in both basins and uses them both. These twin bowls signify, and at the same time invoke, harmony between the high and the low, the sky and the earth and the One who has to unite all human beings.
Provenance: Mali Republic. — Dimensions: diameter of each bowl 0.25 m., height 0.20 m. — Collection: Madame S. de Ganay. — Photographed by Madame S. de Ganay.

Plate XV, 2—2bis

A "doll" for twins (cf. p. 15).
Provenance: Banankoro, Mali Republic. — Material: Wood. — Collection: Beuchelt, Cologne Museum, West Germany. — Photographed by E. Beuchelt.

Plate XVI, 1

Twins' altar, *sinsin* (cf. pp. 13-15). It is suspended in the house porch, like most of the family *boliw* (altars) which must not be in contact with the soil, fire, or water.
Provenance: Konodimini, Mali Republic. — Photographed by Madame S. de Ganay.

Plates XVI, 2—XVII

At Pélenguéna, Mali Republic. The rite to "summon the wind" (cf. p. 15) performed on the "threshing floor of the wind" situated at the eastern end of the threshing floor.

(a) An old mother of twins, crouching with arms crossed, holds in her hands two calabashes full of millet.
(b) The mother of the twins pours out the millet.
(c) The two receptacles are then placed, upside down, near the other tools used for the threshing and winnowing of the millet.
Photographed by Madame S. de Ganay.

Plate XVIII

At Pélenguéna, Mali Republic. Masked dancer of the *n'domo* (cf. pp. 16-17). This personage, with his body completely covered by his robes, represents "ideal man" before his "socialisation". The horns of the mask (the number varies from two to eight according to the masks) are intended to reveal the inner life of the human being.

Photographed by D. Zahan.

Plate XIX

"Walking" mask of the *n'domo*. The leg represents space and the distance covered by walking, thus making it easier for human beings to draw closer together. The foot is the symbol of a foundation and support, of authority and power. Placed behind the lower jaw (which is considered to be the knocker of the mouth, that is the door of speech) these morphological details of the *n'domo* mask signify that speech acquires all its meaning by movement, and by the power which the speaker exercizes over it.

Provenance: Mali Republic. — Dimensions: height 0.60 m., width 0.14 m. — Material: wood of kapok tree. — Collection: D. Zahan. — Photographed by R. Pasquino.

Plate XX

Two *n'domo* masks surrounded by "*n'domo* children".
Provenance: Mali Republic. — Photographed by Madame S. de Ganay.

Plate XXI, 1-2

Two *n'domo* initiates during their flagellation, which is meant to show man's insensibility to suffering, therefore his self-control.
Photographed by Madame S. de Ganay.

Plate XXII

On the threshing floor the *n'domo* mask thrusts his horns into the pile of millet, thus symbolizing man's mortal state.
Photographed by Madame S. de Ganay.

Plate XXIII, 1

Komo mask (cf. pp. 17-18). Two details should be noticed on the *komo* masks, the powerful jaw which represents the hyena (symbol of knowledge, capable of crunching even the hardest bones) and the horns in a position to attack, which again refers to knowledge, said to attack those who take it too lightly.

Provenance: Mali Republic. — Dimensions: 1 m. × 0.30 m. — Material: wood of kapok tree. — Collection: D. Zahan — Photographed by *Musée de l'Homme*.

Plate XXIII, 2

Komo mask
Provenance: Mali Republic. — Dimensions: 1 m. × 0.25 m. — Material: wood of kapok tree. — Private Collection. — Photographed by *Musée de l'Homme*.

Plate XXIV, 1-2

At Douga, Mali Republic. Dance of *Komo* mask.   Photographed by D. Zahan.

Plate XXV, 1

Male *nama* mask (cf. p. 18-19). The two *nama* masks represent the human male and female whose harmonious union is the best protection in the struggle against sorcery.

Provenance: Bélédougou, Mali. Republic — Dimensions: 0.55 m. × 0.15 m. — Material: wood of kapok tree. — Collection: *Musée de l'Homme*. — Photographed by R. Pasquino.

Plate XXV, 2

Female *nama* mask.

Provenance: Bélédougou, Mali Republic. — Dimensions: 0.60 m. × 0.15 m. — Material: wood of kapok tree. — Collection: *Musée de l'Homme*. — Photographed by R. Pasquino.

Plate XXV, 3

Boliw (altars) of *nama*.
Provenance: Mali Republic.

Plate XXVI, 1-2

Sorcery "attachments" (cf. p. 19) hanging from a beam in the men's shelter.
Provenance: Tyongoni, Mali Republic. — Photographed by Madame S. de Ganay.

Plate XXVII, 1

Staves, belonging to the *nama* brotherhood, which are used to discover magic "attachments".
Provenance: Tyongoni, Mali Republic. — Photographed by D. Zahan.

Plate XXVII, 2

Kono mask (cf. p. 19). It represents an elephant (symbol of the intelligence but also of the "volume" of the body of a human being) and also a bird (symbol of thought and spirit).

Provenance: Mali Republic. — Dimensions:. — Material: wood. — Collection: *Musée de l'Homme*. — Photographed by R. Pasquino.

Plate XXVIII, 1

Kono shrine at Tyongoni, Mali Republic. The painting is polychrome: white, red and black. These three colours represent the "foundations" of creation.

Photographed by Madame S. de Ganay.

Plate XXVIII, 2

Zoomorphic *kono* altar.

Provenance: Mali Republic. — Material: terra cotta and wax on wooden frame, the whole coated with coagulated blood. — Collection: *Musée de l'Homme*. — Photographed by H. Tracol.

Plate XXVIII, 3

Zoomorphic *kono* altar.

Provenance: Dyabougou, Mali Republic. — Material: calabash coated with coagulated blood. — Collection: Musée de l'Homme. — Photographed by R. Pasquino.

Plate XXIX

Male mask (to the right) and female mask (to the left) of the *tyiwara* (cf. pp. 20). The former represents the sun, the latter the earth that sustains human beings (represented by the little creature perched on the antelope's back). The association of the two masks, during agrarian ceremonies, evokes the idea of fecundity, wealth and the abundance of the soil penetrated by the sun during the work of farming.

Provenance: Mali Republic. — Photographed by *La Documentation française*, Paris.

Plate XXX

Male *tyiwara* mask. This object, one of the finest in the category, once formed part of the collection of the C. Kjersmeir. Cf. Carl Kjersmeir: *Centres de style de la sculpture nègre africaine*, Paris, 1935-1938.

Plate XXXI

The two *tyiwara* masks dancing in a field in front of the farm workers. No one may pass between the two masks during this exhibition, lest he should place an obstacle between the sun and the earth.

Provenance: Mali Republic. — Cf. M. Delafosse, *Haut-Sénégal-Niger*, vol. III, *Les Civilisations*, p. 32. — Photographed by Fortier.

Plate XXXII, 1

Korè "hyena" mask (cf. p. 22). The figure of this animal (said to be easily duped) represents knowledge in its purely human form, that is, credulous, limited and naive.

Provenance: Mali Republic. — Dimensions: height 0.48 m., width 0.20 m. — Material: wood of kapok tree. — Private collection. — Photographed by D. Zahan.

Plate XXXII, 2

Korè "horse" mask. This object has very profound and complex meanings. The *korè* "horse" is symbolically associated with intelligence, the spirit and intuition. It is also associated with the search for immortality and with the theft of eternity.

Provenance: Mali Republic. — Dimensions: height 0.50 m., width 0.25 m. — Material: wood of kapok tree. — Collection: *Musée de l'Homme*. — Photographed by R. Pasquino.

Plate XXXIII

Korè duga in his ritual "equine" costume. Dressed in this attire, the *korè duga* indulges in wild scampers, leaps and kicks, with desperate gallops which represent man's efforts to attain immortality.

Photographed by M. Griaule.

Plate XXXIV

Flagellation of a *bisa tyila* (cf. p. 22). Flagellation with wooden rods of *Grewia villosa* and *Cissus populnea* symbolises mastery of the tongue (as the organ of speech) and there-fore, power and control over oneself.

Provenance: Diana, Mali Republic. — Photographed by D. Zahan.

Plate XXXV

Group of *bisa tyilaw* showing on their chests the marks of flagellation. Cf. Abbé Henry: *Le culte des Esprits chez les Bambara*, p. 712.

Plate XXXVI, 1

Postulants of the *korè* society ready to be shown into the straw hut ("kitchen") where they are to become divine "food" (cf. p. 44).
Provenance: Diana, Mali Republic. — Photographed by D. Zahan.

Plate XXXVI, 2

The *kala ni* of the *korè*. This object is for the neophytes a means of study as well as an instrument of pedagogy. From the contents of this perch, the novices learn the relation between the elements which it supports and the various categories of the bambara cultural universe, and in this way they fashion for themselves a method of reasoning and a way of "seeing" things which is characteristic of the thought and the civilization of these people.
Provenance: Kouo, Mali Republic. — Photographed by D. Zahan.

Plate XXXVII, 1

A *korè kara* (cf. p. 23). This object represents the deity by means of: a fore-arm (the object's handle) and a hand, the plank itself, with three fingers, index, middle finger and ring finger (adjuncts on the end of the plank); a disproportionately elongated face (part of the plank) containing eyes (the oblong opening), nose (pierced line of chevrons) and mouth (lower oblong opening). The hand and face signify respectively doing and saying, that is, the two most important aspects of wisdom, combined in the same object. This is to show that for the deity (as for the truly wise) speech is never separated from action.
Provenance: Diana, Mali Republic. — Dimensions: 2.50 m. × 0.15 m. — Material wood; polychrome painting (red, black and white). — Photographed by D. Zahan.

Plate XXXVII, 2

An initiate of the *karaw* class of the *korè* reciting the sacred chants of the brotherhood. These chants, composed of verses said to be divinely inspired, express a set of maxims intended to teach the nature of God and the nature of man and to reveal man's privileged relationship with God. They constitute the loftiest expression of the *korè* doctrine, which may rightly be called a mystique.
Provenance: Diana, Mali Republic. — Photographed by D. Zahan.

Plate XXXVIII

A crossroad at Niélé in the Sénoufo region (adjoining the Bambara land), Mali Republic. This drawing (made in 1888, at the time of a geographical mission led by Captain Binger, 1887-1889) seems to prove that a crossroad used to play as important a part in the life of the Sénoufo as it did with the Bambara. Binger relates (p. 245) that "the natives traced cabalistic signs in ashes mixed with water in order to drive away evil spirits". Cf. Captain Binger: *Du Niger au golfe de Guinée*, vol. I, p. 255.

Plate XXXIX, 1

The crossroads, *dangu*, is an important place in Bambara life, especially when it is formed by the intersection of two paths. Its centre then symbolises the initial "point" which was God before, in successive stages, he assumed a shape. It is the transposition of the original crossing of the "paths" which in the beginning of all things the Creator had traced, with his own essence, in order to define space and organize creation. Certain religious manifestations begin and end with a respectful reference to the crossroads. Formerly, in a special case, after the death of a *komo* chief, (whether his death occurred "compulsorily" at the end of his seven years' rule, or during the course of it), his corpse was carried to a crossroads by *komo* initiates. There it was crushed, and the remains were secretly taken to another place. Many purification ceremonies are performed at the sacred crossroads of every village. The offerings to the "spirits" of the bush are left here. The people also deposit here, for a propitiatory purpose, some personal belongings of the defunct, such as the broom and the last spindle of a woman who has recently died.

Ségou Region, Mali Republic. — Photographed by Madame S. de Ganay.

Plate XXXIX, 2

Stone placed on the bank of the Niger during the founding of the village of Banankoro, Mali Republic. Sacrifices are offered here for fishing and agriculture.

Photographed by Madame S. de Ganay.

Plate XL, 1

Sacred pots, *da*, of Massala, and their priest. The *da* generally form an altar dedicated to the earth; oaths concerning the administration of justice are also sworn before them.

Provenance: Mali Republic. — Photographed by Madame S. de Ganay.

Plate XL, 2

Ritual pot placed in the middle of a field belonging to the head of a family. It contains water, as earnest of the humidity needed for the growth of millet, and serves as an altar for sacrifices for agriculture. On these occasions it is filled when the sacrifice is offered and *Faro* is invoked. Then it is covered again, and a little mound of earth is built over it; a little stick is planted in the mound to mark its place. The soil is then watered "so that this field may remain damp'.

Provenance: Ségou region, Mali Republic — Photographed by Madame S. de Ganay.

Plate XLI, 1

Stone of the village fields, common property. Sacrifices are made here in order to obtain abundant crops.

Provenance: Soroba, Mali Republic. — Photographed by Madame S. de Ganay.

Plate XLI, 2

Heap of stones called the "children" of the "common" stone of the village fields. The hoe blade placed on top belongs to the farmer who this year has grown the best crop. A few cowries are placed before the tool as a "reward" to the blade for all its good work.

Provenance: Soroba, Mali Republic. — Photographed by Madame S. de Ganay.

Plate XLII

The distribution of consecrated food after a sacrifice.

Provenance: Mali Republic. — cf. Abbé Henry: *L'Ame d'un peuple africain, les Bambara,* p. 226.

PLATES

Plate I

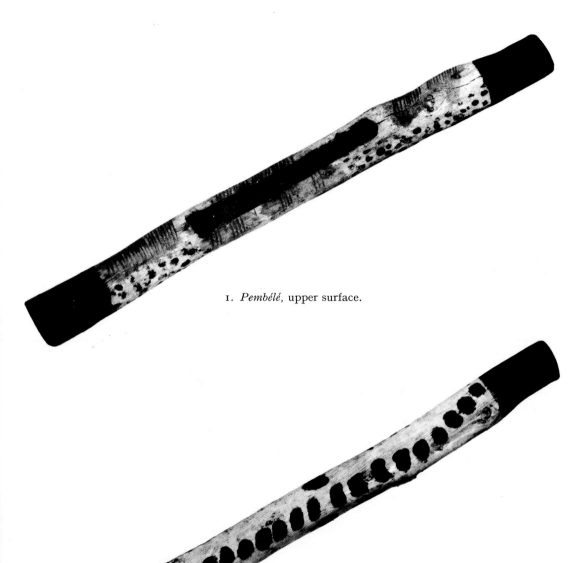

1. *Pembélé*, upper surface.

2. *Pembélé*, lower surface.

Plate II

1. Mask of *Mousso Koroni*.

2. Mask of *Mousso Koroni*.

Plate III

1. Trunk of tree where sacrifices are made to *Mousso koroni*.

2. Calabash of *Faro* water.

Plate IV

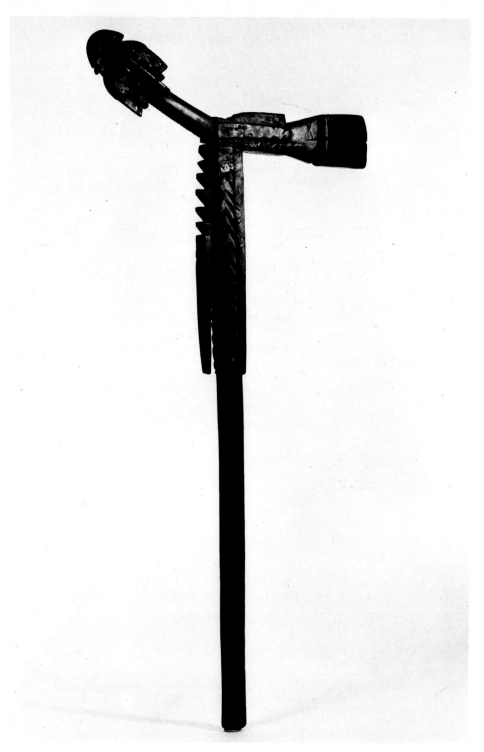

Ritual axe representing androgynous *Faro*.

Plate V

1. Anvil and smith.

2. Common anvil used by all the Kalabougou smiths.

Plate VI

1. Twins' vase.

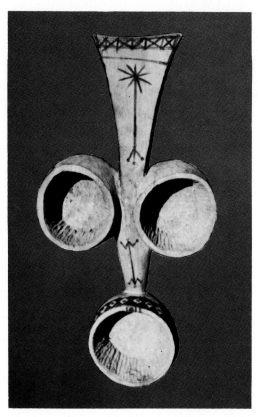

2. Twins' vase.

3. Ancestors' stone.

Plate VII

1. Ancestors' stones.

2. Ancestors' stones.

Plate VIII

1. Tiny "building" dedicated to ancestors, at Kalabougou.

2. Ancestors' altar.

Plate IX

1. Grains, fruits and besoms related to ancestors.

2. Libation of millet gruel.

Plate X

1. Entrance door of a smith's house,
with traces of sacrifice.

2. *Dasiri* tree and animal.

Plate XI

1. (a) Stage in an offering.

2. (b) Stage in an offering.

Plate XII

1. (c) Stage in an offering.

2. (d) Stage in an offering.

Plate XIII

1. (e) Stage in an offering.

2. (f) Stage in an offering.

Plate XIV

(g) Stage in an offering.

Plate XV

1. Female twin's bowl.

2. Twins' doll.

2bis. Twins' doll.

Plate XVI

1. Twins' altar, *sinsin*, hanging in the porch of a house.

2. (a) Rite to "summon the wind".

Plate XVII

1. (b) Rite to "summon the wind".

2. (c) Rite to "summon the wind".

Plate XVIII

Masked *N'domo* dancer.

Plate XIX

"Walking" mask of the *N'domo*.

Plate XX

Two *N'domo* masks.

Plate XXI

Two *N'domo* initiates.

Two *N'domo* initiates.

Plate XXII

On the **threshing** floor the *N'domo* mask thrusts his horns into the pile of millet.

Plate XXIII

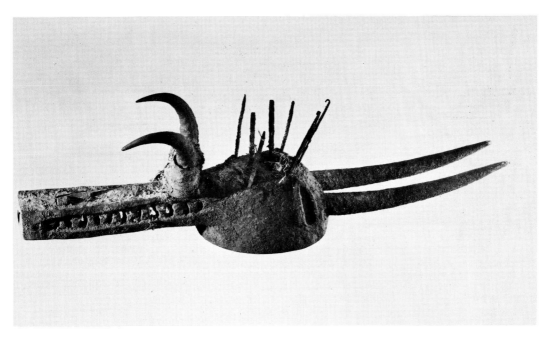

1. *Komo* mask.

2. *Komo* mask.

Plate XXIV

1. *Komo* mask dancing.

2. *Komo* mask dancing.

Plate XXV

1. Male *nama* mask.

2. Female *nama* mask.

3. *Boliw* (altars) of the *nama*.

Plate XXVI

1. Sorcery "attachments".

2. Sorcery "attachments".

Plate XXVII

1. Staves of the *nama* brotherhood.

2. *Kono* mask.

Plate XXVIII

1. *Kono* shrine.

2. Zoomorphic altar of the *kono*.

3. Zoomorphic altar of the *kono*.

Plate XXIX

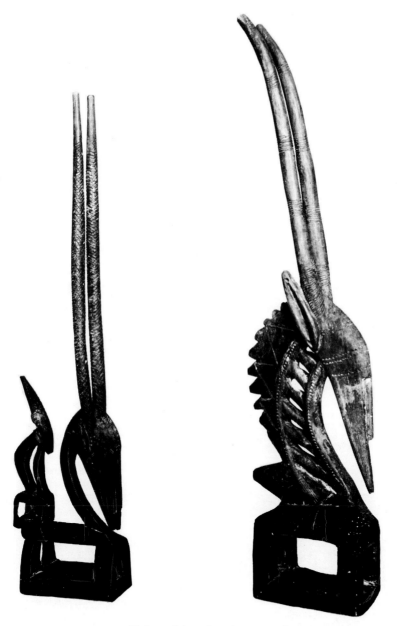

Male and female *tyiwara* masks.

Plate XXX

Male *tyiwara* mask.

Plate XXXI

The two *tyiwara* masks.

Plate XXXII

1. *Korè* "hyena" mask.

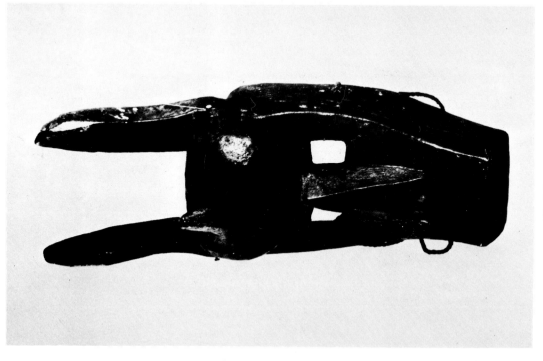

2. *Korè* "horse" mask.

Plate XXXIII

Korè duga in his ritual "equine" costume.

Plate XXXIV

Flagellation of a *bisa tyila*.

Plate XXXV

Group of *bisa tyilaw*.

Plate XXXVI

1. Postulants of the *korè* society.

2. The *kala ni* of the *korè*.

Plate XXXVII

2. An initiate of the *karaw* class of the *korè*.

1. A *kara* of the *korè*.

Plate XXXVIII

Crossroads at *Niélé*.

Plate XXXIX

1. Crossroads, *dangu*, an important place in the Bambara world.

2. Stone placed on the Niger bank.

Plate XL

1. Sacred pots, *da*, and their priest.

2. Ritual pottery.

Plate XLI

1. Stone of the village fields, common property.

2. Heap of stones called "children" of the "common" stone of the village fields.

Plate XLII

Distribution of consecrated food.